The
Philo
TRUST
Transforming lives

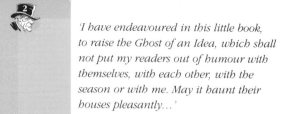

'I have endeavoured in this little book,
to raise the Ghost of an Idea, which shall
not put my readers out of humour with
themselves, with each other, with the
season or with me. May it haunt their
houses pleasantly…'
Charles Dickens, December 1843

I once saw a sign outside a
church that was like this one,
it really made me smile!
Times are changing! Today,
we live in a multi-faith, multi-
cultural society, and that sign
said it all. Our society is like
a melting pot, with all sorts of
cultural and religious flavours
thrown in, stirred around, and
seasoned to personal taste.

VARIETY – THE SPICE OF LIFE?

Today, many people have developed a consumerist way of seeing religion, in which they 'pick and mix' their favourite faiths and spirituality like a selection of sweets.

But even though I quite enjoy variety, I don't completely buy the consumerist way when it comes to spiritual faith. Christianity, which began with the birth of Jesus in a stable in Bethlehem, comes with a price.

The Good News is that it's a price money could never buy…

"God does not play dice with the universe".
Albert Einstein

Christmas is here again, the festival that
calls from its ancient past to our present.
You might feel that you are familiar with
the story, that you know it and that you
don't need to take another look.

But we can all get so
used to things that
we ignore the detail.
We think we know
what it's all about,
but do we really?

The average debt
run up at Christmas
is £323, ranging
from less than £20
to over £1000.

On average we
spend 15.2 hours
Christmas shopping.
Women spend more
time shopping than
men, with women
spending an average
19.4 hours shopping,
compared to men
spending 10.9 hours.

Take Charles Dickens' *A Christmas Carol*. Published in 1843, it's one of the best-loved stories to be set at this time of year.

We probably think we know the story back to front. After all, it's been adapted into over 200 films, and is such a powerful tale that it's credited with helping to define our contemporary understanding of Christmas.

BAH HUMBUG!

A fresh look at this all-time classic, reminds us that it's far more than just a feel-good festive tale featuring an old miser with a memorable catchphrase. In fact, the story of Ebenezer Scrooge and his tormenting spirits helps us to consider what is of eternal value, here in the 21st century. For that reason alone, it's worth a closer inspection.

Dickens set out to persuade his readers to summon the spirit of Christmas not just for a week in December, but also for all the year round. His message, sent deep from within the 19th century, strikes a chord with us today. It has a timeless, universal quality, like all the best works of art.

Oliver Cromwell's parliament abolished Christmas in 1647. In 1660, with a King back on the throne, Christmas was reinstated.

The star at the top of the Christmas tree represents the star which (recorded in the Bible) appeared above the stable in Bethlehem where Jesus Christ was born.

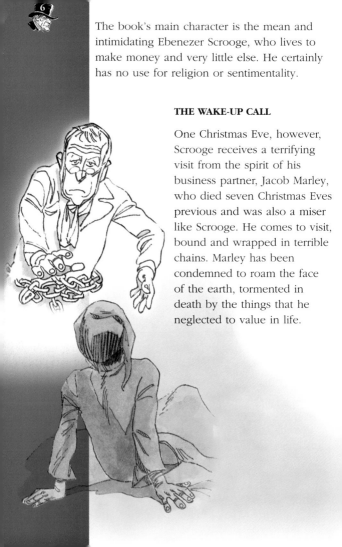

The book's main character is the mean and intimidating Ebenezer Scrooge, who lives to make money and very little else. He certainly has no use for religion or sentimentality.

THE WAKE-UP CALL

One Christmas Eve, however, Scrooge receives a terrifying visit from the spirit of his business partner, Jacob Marley, who died seven Christmas Eves previous and was also a miser like Scrooge. He comes to visit, bound and wrapped in terrible chains. Marley has been condemned to roam the face of the earth, tormented in death by the things that he neglected to value in life.

He is desperate to give his old colleague a final chance to avoid the same fate.

'My spirit never walked beyond our counting house,' he warns Scrooge. *'My spirit never roved beyond the narrow limits of our money changing hole…'* This, he makes clear, is Scrooge's last opportunity to turn from his ignorant, selfish, insular ways. Marley's spirit instructs him to wait for three more spirits of Christmas past, present and future. Reluctantly, Scrooge understands that this is for real, as he sees Marley float away to join a crowd of tormented souls who are wailing and moaning in the night sky.

On the stroke of one o'clock, the spirit of Christmas Past arrives, and draws back the curtain from around Scrooge's bed to reveal his face. He takes him on an unforgettable trip down memory lane, on a visit to his own childhood. Scrooge is astonished to see old, familiar faces playing happily in the open air. As the spirit takes him into a schoolroom, however, they see a lonely little boy sitting by the fire, whose only companion is the book he is reading.

ICM Survey of children aged 7-12
When asked to agree or disagree with the question: *"It's better to earn less money but have more time with your family"*, 77% of children polled, opted for more time and less money.

Scrooge remembers his loneliness, and how he longed for the presence and warmth of friends. He recalls his past desires for the love and approval of his family, but then sees all the people who tried to reach out to him, who attempted to stop his slide into self-absorption and an increasing preoccupation with personal security.

He sees his former fiancée, Belle, who came a poor second to Scrooge's passion for wealth. *'A golden idol displaces me,'* she complains to him. *'All hopes have merged to a master passion; the thought of money engrosses you!'*

A ROOT OF ALL EVIL?

Dickens explores, through Scrooge's terrifying ordeal, the love of money compared with the value of relationships. Scrooge's whole life has come to revolve around his counting house. His insatiable appetite consumes him for more.

To him, Christmas has become nothing more than a 'time for finding yourself a year older, and not an hour richer'.

BACK TO THE FUTURE

Back in the 21st century, we can fall into a similar trap, seeing money – and the things it can buy – as the answer to our problems. Especially if our lives have not been that happy, like the young Ebenezer Scrooge. We perceive the 'good life' as being about an abundance of bigger, brighter and better things. And if we start to feel guilty, we can excuse ourselves with the thought that we want our children to have the things we missed out on.

Jacob Marley's ghostly visit is not just a wake up call for Scrooge. As we hear his words, we should make sure that we haven't lost out on the things that money can't buy. We all need money, of course – but it's possible to pay too high a price for it. It's as if society has caught a cultural disease called 'affluenza'. The symptoms include always wanting more, despite what we already have.

And then there's the insatiable desire for 'success' without experiencing contentment. Consistently, we choose our career over family. And we seem unwilling to settle for less than the best of everything.

If Scrooge has been shaken by the visit of the first spirit, then the second is no less disturbing. The Spirit of Christmas Present arrives to take Scrooge on a tour of the people he now knows.

"Content makes poor men rich. Discontent makes rich men poor".
Benjamin Franklin

12

CHRISTMAS CHEER?

Joseph Rowntree Foundation:
10,000 people die every year in the UK because they are poor. Among these are 1,400 children.

Scrooge finds himself standing in the home of his poor clerk, Bob Cratchit, where he feels the warmth of a large and friendly family who are making the best of what little they can afford on the small salary Scrooge pays. He experiences their anxiety over the fate of Tiny Tim, the Cratchit's sick youngest child.

Scrooge is clearly shown the effects of his selfish nature; but the spirit helps him understand that even though he is utterly hard-hearted, others have not entirely given up on him. As they sit down to their feeble Christmas dinner, Bob Cratchit thinks to toast his boss, despite protests from his wife.

The Foundation suggests that the number of premature deaths could be cut by 7,500 each year if inequalities in income and wealth were tackled and returned to their 1983 levels.

In England in 2001 there were 184,290 families that were homeless. The charity Shelter estimates that this represents over 440,000 people including 100,000 children. It is not known how many single people or couples without children are homeless.

The Spirit of Christmas Present then shows Scrooge the harsh reality of life on the streets, together with the absolute determination of the families who live there to stay out of the prisons and workhouses, whatever the cost. Scrooge has never before seen the need to help anyone other than himself.

He's always believed that the poor 'should go to the institutions provided – if they should rather die, let them die and reduce the surplus population'. But his heart is softening…

"Remember the end never really justifies the meanness!"

Anon

SUFFER THE LITTLE CHILDREN?

Then, the Spirit reveals two hauntingly thin and deathly children from within his cloak. They are called IGNORANCE and WANT – two of the grim realities of Victorian life. The Spirit describes them as the 'children of all who walk the earth unseen'. On their brow is written 'DOOM'.

But it is not the quivering, hollow children who are doomed. As Scrooge pleads for them to be removed from his sight, the Spirit explains that 'doom spells the downfall of you and all those who deny their existence.'

"Love is the basic need
of human nature,
for without it life is
disrupted emotionally,
mentally, spiritually
and physically."

Dr Karl Menninger

MIRROR MIRROR

Before you put someone in his or her place,
you should put yourself in theirs. How much
poverty do we allow ourselves to see?
The Spirit responds, *'They are hidden, but
they live.'* Dickens holds a mirror not just to
Scrooge's face, but also to ours. How do we
treat the poor, the weak and the vulnerable?
Do we allow our lifestyles to shield us from
the needs of the poor and downtrodden?

After all, we are not on this earth to see through one another, but to see one another through.

FUTURE SHOCK

"Misers are no fun to live with, but they make great ancestors."

Tom Snyder

Then comes the final spirit, the Spirit of Christmas Future, who has no face and does not speak. It merely points.

Scrooge looks to where the spirit is leading him, and sees the Cratchit family again, worn down in their struggle against poverty, and now without Tiny Tim, who has died for lack of proper medical care.

"Although the world is full of suffering, it is full also of the overcoming of it."
Helen Keller

The Spirit takes Scrooge to visit the house
of a man who has died in his sleep.
A maid and a cleaner are dividing up his
belongings before the undertaker arrives.

Two associates out in the street are
discussing whether it's even necessary
to hold a funeral service, since no one
would bother to come.

'But who is this man?' asks the miser.

The spirit leads him to a grave, whose headstone bears the name 'Ebenezer Scrooge'. It's a chilling reminder that no one lives forever; that the journey of life is brief. As the Bible says, *'our days on earth are as a shadow'* 1 Chronicles 29.15

"I have long considered it one of God's greatest mercie that the future is hidden from us. If it weren't, life would surely be unbearable."

Eugene Forsey

HERE LIES EBENEZER SCROOGE

We have all been given another opportunity, because of the birth of the hero of the greatest Christmas story, Jesus Christ."

The spirit asks Scrooge to consider himself from God's perspective: *'It may be that in heaven's sight you are more worthless and less fit to live than millions like this man's child.'* What is more valuable in God's eyes?

This is it, the life-changing moment when Scrooge understands that it's now or never. He asks whether it's possible to mend his ways and so alter his life and destiny. Surely the Spirits wouldn't be visiting him if not?

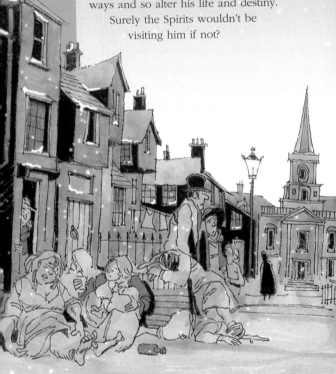

As Christmas morning dawns and he wakes,
once more, to the world, Scrooge realises that
he has been given a reprieve. He has another
opportunity to be more human – just as
Dickens believed we have all been
given another opportunity,
because of the birth of the
hero of the greatest
Christmas story,
Jesus Christ.

"You are free to choose, but the choices that you make will determine what you will have, be and do in the tomorrows of your life."

Many of us will recognise the struggles
of Ebenezer Scrooge in our own lives.
Many of us have been hurt as we grew up.
Many of us pass up the offer of friendship
or kindness out of a fear of rejection.
Scrooge was a man who lived in a prison
of his own making, the doors shut and sealed
with a bitterness, which he would not let go.

In fact, Dickens symbolises the consequence
of our selfish actions by the chain that traps
Jacob Marley's spirit and weighs him down.
Marley tells Scrooge that he alone forged it in
life: *'I made it, link by link and yard by yard.'*

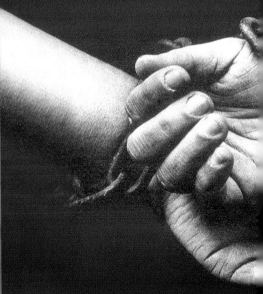

His chains were forged with regrets,
which he could not release, and hurts
he would not forgive. And as he stands
before Scrooge, he can see the even
greater chains that bind his old colleague:
*'Would you know the weight and length
of the coil you bear yourself?'* asks Marley.
*'It was full as heavy and as long as
this, seven Christmas Eves ago.
You have laboured on it since.
It is a ponderous chain.'*

> "Everyone says
> forgiveness is a good
> idea, until they have
> something to forgive."
>
> C.S. Lewis

"Change is the law of life and those who look only to the past or present are certain to miss the future."

John F. Kennedy

GOOD NEWS FOR A CHANGE

The good news is that we can learn from the past, to change now so that we can create a better future. Just as the spirits of Christmas wanted Scrooge to change for good, so God knows us better than we know ourselves, and loves us enough to help us to change and make a difference.

Christmas is the time and place where God draws back the curtain, so we can see his face. Jesus has come to free us, because we are bound by chains. In fact, because of Jesus, we can commemorate the past, consecrate the present and contemplate the future. Jesus came to give us a new outlook on life.

The good news is that we, like Scrooge, are still alive. It's not too late: we can choose to change. Life can only be understood backwards, but it must be lived forwards. Whatever our past has been, we can have a better future.

At the heart of 'A Christmas Carol' lies Scrooge's transformation. From a selfish, greedy and bitter old man, we see him become a grateful, generous and compassionate figure.

A man filled with deep regret sees his life transformed, to the point where Dickens concludes he became as good a friend, as good a master, and as good a man, as the good old city knew.'

Things do not change. We do. Scrooge learns his lesson, and he experiences what amounts to a 'conversion'. He responds by changing his ways and living out the lessons that he learnt on that Christmas Eve. He repents and changes his destiny.

"Progress is impossible without change; and those who can't change their minds cannot change anything."
George Bernard Shaw

"Never does the human soul appear so strong and noble as when it foregoes revenge and dares to forgive an injury."

E.H.Chapin

"The weak can never forgive. Forgiveness is the attribute of the strong."

Mahatma Gandhi

Jesus, the Son of God, invites us to do the same. What better time than Christmas to receive forgiveness, renew our faith, release our fears and rebuild friendships? Faith, after all, is made real in thought, word and deed.

In case you are still making a Christmas list, here are some timeless gifts that won't cost you anything, except perhaps, a little pride. You could mend a quarrel, release a grudge, lessen your demands on others, apologise, forgive someone who has treated you wrongly, find a forgotten friend, write an overdue thank-you note, point out one thing you appreciate most about someone you live or work with, dismiss suspicion, tell someone you love them, or give something away. You cannot do a kindness too soon, because you never know how soon it will be too late.

We talk about 'the birth of new ideas' and of hope being 'born' in the human heart. Why not let Jesus be born into your life, this Christmas time?

It takes a conscious, personal decision to become a follower of Jesus, which begins by acknowledging that we all need Him – to forgive us for what we have done wrong, and to guide us into real life, the life He promised to give us 'to the full'.

"Peace if possible, truth at all costs."
Martin Luther

In our consumer culture, Jesus isn't just another pick-and-mix lifestyle guru; in fact, he claimed exclusively to be 'the Way, the Truth and the Life'. If we choose to follow him, then we also have to count the cost – of dedication, commitment, perseverance, selfless love and generosity.

But the reward – a dynamic, living relationship with the dynamic, living God – is surely worth it.

If you want to make this Christmas one to remember, then there's no need to wait any longer. If you ask Jesus to forgive your past, and invite him to enter your Christmas present, then your life will be transformed – now, and for good.

Dickens sent a message to us in the form of an amazing story. God sends his message in the form of his Son, Jesus Christ, who lives today. In the words of the wonderful carol 'O Little Town of Bethlehem', we can actually invite Jesus to be with us, like he was, all those years ago at the first Christmas:

*'O holy Child of Bethlehem,
descend to us, we pray;
Cast out our sin, and enter in,
be born in us today.
We hear the Christmas angels
the great glad tidings tell;
O come to us, abide with us,
our Lord
Emmanuel!'*

"I would not say I believe. I know. I have had the experience of being gripped by something that is stronger than myself, something that people call God."

Carl Jung

May God grant you the light of Christmas,
which is faith;
The warmth of Christmas,
which is love;
The radiance of Christmas,
which is purity;
The righteousness of Christmas,
which is justice;
The belief in Christmas,
which is truth;
The all of Christmas,
which is Christ.

As we celebrate the birth of Jesus,
may God grant you all these things
– not just at Christmas, but throughout
the New Year and all the years to come.

"The supreme
happiness in life,
is the conviction
that we are
loved."

Victor Hugo

Copyright © 2004
The Philo Trust
141 High Street
Rickmansworth
Herts WD3 1AR
UK

Credits

Design and Illustrations by:
Pete Goddard and Bob Bond © 2004 The Philo Trust
Words copyright © 2004 J John

Photographs kindly provided by:
Christian Publicity Organisation © 2004
    Pages 4 (bottom), 26, 28, 31
Getty Images © 2004
    Pages 4 (top), 10
Jubilee Campaign © 2004
    Pages 24/25
NSPCC © 2004
    Page 14
Shelter © 2004
    Page 17

Published in the UK by:
Verité CM Ltd
124 Sea Place,
Worthing BN12 4BG

ISBN: 1-904726-01-1

Printed and bound in England